Some hamsters are timid little creatures, frightened of their own shadows, but not Hannibal! When chance throws him headlong into the strange and dangerous world outside his cage, he welcomes the opportunity to explore. The terrifyingly narrow escape from Owl, the friendly advice of Rabbit, the dire warning from Seagull he takes in his stride, learning as he goes along which creatures to trust and which to fear. But at the end of each adventure he is glad when rescue comes and he can return to the comfort and safety of his own home.

Hannibal runs away

Story by Raymond Howe
Illustrations by John Berry

Ladybird Books Ltd
Loughborough
1976

HANNIBAL RUNS AWAY

Hannibal the hamster was unhappy. He lived in a little wooden cage in the corner of the tool shed, and his life was so dull! Nothing exciting ever happened to him.

Like all hamsters, Hannibal slept all day long. When it was dusk he woke up, and stretched his paws, and yawned, and twitched his whiskers – surely tonight, he thought, something exciting would happen to him at last. But nothing ever did.

One night he made up his mind to run away. First he had to gnaw a hole in his cage. This was quite easy, for he had good strong teeth. He gnawed steadily all through the night. When morning came he covered the hole he had made with a pile of hay, and settled down to sleep.

In the middle of the second night the hole was big enough for him to squeeze through. His great adventure had begun!

All at once he felt afraid. He was leaving his cosy cage, the only home he had ever known. Was it wise?

In a moment he had quite forgotten his fear. He simply slipped out of his cage and ran towards the side of the tool shed, looking for a way out.

He came across the entrance to a tunnel which was just his size, and which seemed to lead in the direction he wanted to go. He was in so much of a hurry to be on his way that he did not think that the tunnel might belong to someone else. He had hardly scrambled into the entrance when he met Field Mouse, hurrying into the shelter of the tool shed.

"Goodness! How you frightened me!" said Field Mouse. He was a timid fellow.

There was not room to pass in the narrow tunnel, and Hannibal was quite certain that HE would not give way. So Field Mouse had to turn back the way he had come. Hannibal followed close behind.

Presently Field Mouse said, "Shh . . . be very quiet. We're coming out." Hannibal was excited. He couldn't see why it was necessary to be so quiet, and Field Mouse had slowed down so much that they were hardly moving at all. What was causing the delay? Why didn't the fellow get a move on?

They came out at last into bright moonlight. Hannibal had never seen anything so wonderful. There was grass beneath his feet, cool soft grass which smelled so sweet, and which would surely be lovely to scamper on. But Field Mouse would go no further.

"Come out, come out and play!" shouted Hannibal in delight. "What are you afraid of?"

"I'm afraid of Owl," said Field Mouse. "Owl may be lurking near."

"Who is Owl?" asked Hannibal. "I've never heard of him."

"Owl is the silent enemy," answered Field Mouse. "Silent and ghostly in the moonlight – no one has seen him clearly and lived to tell it. Swift as the wind he comes and goes. Beware of his shadow.
If it falls upon you, run!
Do not turn to look.
Run quickly and hide – then
perhaps you will be safe."

Hannibal thought, what nonsense Field Mouse does talk. Why, there is nothing out there. Nothing except the moonlight, and the murmur of the wind in the leaves, and the fresh green grass.

He went boldly out to play.

The last words of Field Mouse came to him, just a faint squeak carried by the night air. Hannibal was hardly listening.

"Goodbye," called Field Mouse. "Look for the Black Log. It is a haven, a place of safety. You will find food and shelter at the Black Log. Goodbye . . ."

Hannibal was far out in the middle of the grassy space, dancing merrily in the moonlight. He was free at last, and life was suddenly a grand game. Once, he saw a shadow on the ground, a little way ahead of where he was dancing, but it was only a white rock. It glowed with light, and it cast a deep black shadow, but it did not move.

Hannibal wandered here and there, following tiny paths in the grass, not caring where they led him.

"After all," he thought, "I have plenty of time." He had really grown very careless.

As he came near to the white rock he heard a gentle 'Whoosh'. He thought it was just a stronger breeze, but no! It was a huge shadow, and it was racing towards him. At once, he remembered the words of Field Mouse, and he knew he was in danger. Owl was hunting tonight.

Hannibal dived straight for the white rock. Luckily there was a small hollow underneath it. Hannibal pushed himself inside, but he was not quite quick enough. There was a sound of tearing fur. Hannibal squealed in pain. He felt the swish! of wings close by, and he turned and looked into Owl's face.

Owl had two big saucer eyes, and a great head, and wide shadowy wings that sped away across the field. He was gone. Hannibal was alone.

He shivered in fear beneath the white rock. His body ached. His head was spinning. He wished he had never left his cage.

Presently he crept out of his hiding place and walked slowly up the hill. Just as he was feeling very unhappy, and sore, and hungry, he came to the top of the grassy bank.

Down below him he saw Woody Pool and there, beside the water, stood a big black log.

He ran all the way down the hill, and crawled into a hollow underneath Black Log. He found a few sweet brown beech nuts for his supper, and when he had eaten them, he curled into a tight little ball, twitched his whiskers once, and fell asleep.

When Hannibal woke up, it was late in the afternoon. The sun was shining through the leaves of the trees that grew near to Woody Pool. Hannibal blinked and stretched his paws. Then he sat up and washed his face. After that, he felt better. He was just about to leave his place beneath Black Log when he noticed another small creature watching him. It was Stag Beetle.

"Hello," said Stag Beetle brightly. "Did you sleep well?"

"Indeed I did," replied Hannibal. "Thank you for asking."

"That's all right," said Stag Beetle. Then he introduced himself. "By the way," he said, "I'm Stag Beetle, and I'm pleased to meet you."

"I'm pleased to meet you, too," said Hannibal politely. "My – you are very smart and shiny."

"This is my armour," said Stag Beetle proudly, turning his black body so that the sunlight shone on his fine polished coat. "It quite often saves me from my enemies."

Hannibal thought of Owl. "Does Owl hunt near Woody Pool?" he asked.

"Yes," replied Stag Beetle. "But I'm rather too small for Owl to bother with, I think. *I* have to watch out for Hedgehog."

Hannibal wondered what Hedgehog looked like. "Shall I meet him too?" he asked.

"Yes," said Stag Beetle. "He wakes up at night, like you. That's why I must stay very close to Black Log."

"I understand," said Hannibal. "Will you excuse me now? I must go to the pool to drink."

"Of course," said Stag Beetle. "Goodbye."

By the time Hannibal had made his way carefully back to the pool, it was quite dark. He wondered whether Stag Beetle was still waiting under Black Log – but he would never know, because Stag Beetle was so black he could not be seen in the darkness.

All at once there was a rustling, scraping sound among the grass and dry leaves nearby. Hannibal crouched down and kept very quiet. Then out of the gloom there appeared a spikey little ball, from which an inquisitive pointed head poked. Hannibal knew this must be Hedgehog.

"Hello," said Hedgehog, in a gruff voice. "You are a stranger here. Why do you come to Black Log ?"

Hannibal had never met a hedgehog before. He was very frightened by such a strong greeting, but he made up his mind to speak bravely.

"I came to Black Log to look for adventure," he said. "Life is very boring."

"Life boring! At your age!" snorted Hedgehog. "When I was your age . . ." He sighed. "If you're looking for adventure, then follow the path over the hill, but beware the wide road."

"What is the wide road?" asked Hannibal.

"The wide road leads to town," said Hedgehog. "It carries roaring monsters, which will crush you." He became sad, and his voice softened. "Many of my kind got bored with life and moved on, only to perish on the wide road," he said. "Even our strong spines will not protect us from the roaring monsters who hunt along the road."

"Thank you," said Hannibal. "I will be careful."

"Good luck to you, stranger," said Hedgehog. "The time of the Yellow Leaves is here. I am ready for my sleep. You, too, must find a place to rest before the leaves fall."

With that, Hedgehog moved off. His short legs carried him away very quickly. Soon there was only the sound of him as he scraped through the dead leaves.

A big yellow moon had risen. Beyond the clump of trees round Woody Pool, it shone and lit the hillside. Hannibal set off. He was more careful now. He went slowly on his way, keeping a look out for Owl, and any other enemies who might be hunting in the field. He journeyed for more than half the night, and he met no one. At last he came safely to the edge of the golden wheatfield.

Beside the path there were several large ears of

wheat. Hannibal ate until he could eat no more, and then stuffed his cheek-pouches so full of the ripe grain that they bulged out to twice their normal size.

Just as he was about to move along the path into the middle of the field, Rabbit came running towards him. Rabbit was very large, and he was always in a hurry. His fur gleamed silver in the moonlight and his long ears were pricked up, listening and alert.

"I heard you coming through the stubble," said Rabbit, "and I must know all that is happening in this part of the field. I have to run and warn my friends in the warren when danger comes."

"Don't worry," said Hannibal. "I'm very small – too small to harm a rabbit, even if I wanted to. I came for the ripe wheat."

"Help yourself," said Rabbit. "You are welcome. There is plenty for everyone."

"Thank you," said Hannibal. "My pouches are already full."

Rabbit flicked his ears and turned away. "I'll be off, then," he said. "I should be glad to show you around the wheatfield, any time."

"No, thank you," said Hannibal. "You are much taller than I am, and you can see over the stubble – but if I went wandering there I should get lost. I must stay on the path."

"If I can help you, I will," said Rabbit.

"I am following the way to the wide road," said Hannibal.

Rabbit trembled in fear. "Keep to the path then," he said. "Go out of the field by the great gate – the road is just beyond the great gate. If you can get there at dawn you will be safe. The roaring monsters are sleeping in the hour before dawn. They will not harm you then."

"Thank you," said Hannibal. "Is there a place to sleep ?"

"Hide in the Wood Pile," said Rabbit. "I have a burrow there. It is a good place to sleep. Goodbye . . ."

The path which Hannibal was following had been made by the wheel of a tractor. It was quite straight and the centre of it was made of hard, flattened earth. There were deep ridges of soil on both sides of the path, and over the top of these, Hannibal could just see the first rows of stubble beyond.

That night, Hannibal travelled so far that by the time the sun rose, he was very tired. As the sky lit up and the stars vanished one by one, Hannibal could see the end of the path. He scrambled over the last of the dry earth, and then he was suddenly at the top of a gentle rise. Great black shadows appeared, and where they fell, the golden wheat-stubble was darkened. Hannibal looked up; the shadows came from the great gate; he had arrived at the end of the field.

The great gate was made of wood, and it towered so high above the tiny hamster that at first he thought it filled the whole sky. But it did not block his way. He passed underneath the big wooden bars quite easily.

Beyond the gate, Hannibal was suddenly lost in high grass. All through the summer, the grass had never been cut. Now it had grown tall, and the stalks were swaying and rustling in the wind. Hannibal went on.

Suddenly, the grass ended. Hannibal tumbled out, rolled head-over-heels down a steep bank, and landed on the wide road.

He picked himself up, shook the dust from his fur, and looked up. He could see a long, long way. The surface of the road was hard and shiny and black. It had a strange smell. Hannibal trembled. Where were the roaring monsters? What if one of them should spring upon him now? "I must find the Wood Pile," he thought.

Luckily, the Wood Pile was quite close. It reminded him of Black Log; but the Wood Pile was made up of many logs, and it rose up almost as high as the great gate.

Hannibal soon found Rabbit's burrow. Just above the opening of the burrow, among the logs, he found a nest of leaves. He hid his store of wheat under the leaves. Then he slept.

When he woke up, the sun was shining brightly. A strange noise was coming from somewhere nearby.

Hannibal looked outside. One of the roaring monsters was standing beside the Wood Pile; but it wasn't roaring. It seemed to be purring, and then suddenly it stopped, and became quiet. Hannibal heard another sound, and this time it was one that he had heard before. A man's voice said quite

clearly, “Well – better get this lot loaded up, I suppose.” Another man answered, “All right – wait a minute – I’ll help you.”

The log on which Hannibal was sitting began to move. It swung up in the air, and landed with a clang inside the roaring monster. Several other logs fell near to Hannibal, but luckily none of them hit him.

Soon afterwards, the roaring monster began to growl, and then it was moving along the wide road. Hannibal wasn't afraid. In some way that he could not understand, he felt it was right for him to be in the company of men. The wide fields had frightened him much more. He knew he could never belong with Field Mouse, Hedgehog, and the rest of the wild creatures.

At last they reached the town. The roaring monster stopped. (It was not a living thing, of course. It was just a big lorry.) When the wood was unloaded, Hannibal ran quickly away.

It happened that there was a garden near to the place where the wood was stored. Hannibal found his way into the garden. It was still mid-day when he arrived, and he had to find a place to hide. In one corner of the garden there stood a big wooden box. It was similar to the tool shed where Hannibal had begun his journey, but it was propped up on four wooden legs, and there was a space underneath which was just the right spot for Hannibal to hide in for the rest of the day. Not only was the wooden box a perfect shelter – there were a few ears of wheat underneath, too. Hannibal ate a good lunch, and settled down to wait for the night-time.

When the sun had set, and the garden was dusky, Hannibal decided it was time to have a look around. He crept out from his hiding place. Suddenly, he was startled by a cluck! cluck! – and a great scratching – and then another voice.

"I'm Bertie the bantam. I heard you, creeping about underneath my coop. I thought for a moment you were Cat, but I can see that you are only a mouse."

"Good evening," said Hannibal. "But – I'm not a mouse. I'm a hamster."

"It doesn't matter what you are," said Bertie the bantam. "Cat will not care whether you are rat, mouse, or hamster."

"Who is Cat?" asked Hannibal.

"Cat is a fearful creature," replied Bertie the bantam. "But I have no time for more talking. It is late. Goodnight."

And he went off to his coop.

By the time midnight came, Hannibal had explored most of the garden. There was no one in sight. The human beings and the bantams were fast asleep. There were one or two snails near to a damp wall, but Hannibal did not think that they were interesting enough to talk to.

He was making his way steadily back towards the bantam coop, when Cat pounced.

Cat was so huge that Hannibal couldn't believe what he saw. Two green eyes seemed to be hanging in the sky like lamps. Although Cat was black, he had one white paw, and this one single paw alone was nearly as big as Hannibal.

How Cat missed him with that first pounce Hannibal never knew. But he had learned many things in the wild fields, and now he raced for cover. Just in time, he slid under the bantam coop. But Cat still didn't give up. The great white paw followed Hannibal until he squeezed flat into the farthest corner. Cat bared his claws.

All at once there was a dreadful barking. Dog had discovered that Cat was in his garden.

Dog and Cat met outside the bantam coop. They had a very noisy quarrel, and Hannibal was forgotten. At last the hissing of Cat and the barking of Dog were both silenced by the voice of a man.

"Patch! Be quiet, now! Come here!" called the man. Then, in a quieter voice, he said, "I really can't understand what all the fuss is about – but I do believe there's something under the bantam coop."

Another voice, a woman's, said, "I'll fetch the torch, and we'll have a look."

The white beam of the torch shone into Hannibal's eyes, nearly blinding him for a moment. The lady stretched her hand towards him. "Well," she said, "it's not a rat, and it's not a mouse. Why – I do believe it's a hamster. I wonder where it has come from?"

Hannibal nestled in the lady's hand. It was a gentle hand, and it smelled good.

The next day there was a great storm. Hannibal watched it from inside the house. He had been given a new cage, and there was fresh hay for him to sleep in, and good food for him to eat. Through the window of the house he could see that the wind was blowing all the leaves down from the trees in the garden. They were dead leaves – yellow and brown and dead, they settled in piles on the lawn; and Hannibal remembered the words of Hedgehog. He knew that he had found a good place to spend the winter.

By now Hedgehog would surely be curled up among the dry leaves underneath Black Log. And what about Stag Beetle, and Field Mouse, and the rest of the wild creatures?

Hannibal remembered them all; and he thought about the part each one of them had played in his great adventure.

It had all been very wonderful; and the most wonderful thing of all was that now he had found a new home; a home where he knew he would be cared for.

"I shall never need to run away again," he thought, happily.

He stretched his paws, twitched his whiskers once, and fell asleep.